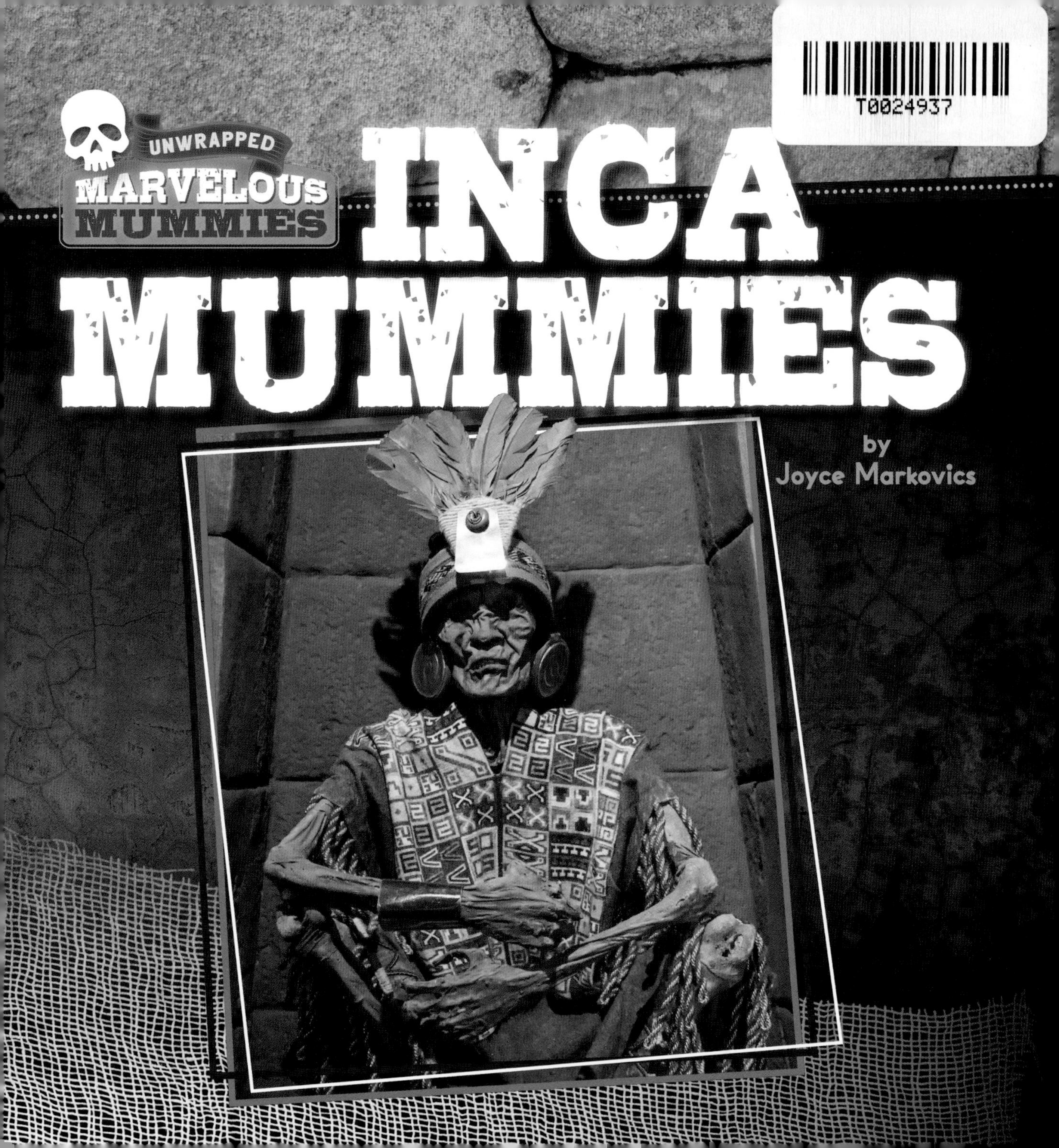
UNWRAPPED
MARVELOUS MUMMIES
INCA MUMMIES
by
Joyce Markovics

CHERRY LAKE PRESS

Published in the United States of America by Cherry Lake Publishing Group
Ann Arbor, Michigan
www.cherrylakepublishing.com

Reading Adviser: Marla Conn, MS Ed., Literacy specialist, Read-Ability, Inc.
Content Adviser: Owen Beattie, PhD
Book Designer: Ed Morgan

Photo Credits: © pablopicasso/Shutterstock, cover and title page; © Milton Rodriguez/Shutterstock, TOC; © Porky Pies Photography/Alamy Stock Photo, 4–5; © Johan Reinhard, 5; © Johan Reinhard, 6; © Johan Reinhard, 7; © freepik.com, 8–9; © lovelypeace/Shutterstock, 9; © Anton Watman/Shutterstock, 10; Wikimedia Commons, 11; © Johan Reinhard, 12; Wikimedia Commons, 13; © matin/Shutterstock, 13 right; Wikimedia Commons, 14; © Johan Reinhard, 15; © Johan Reinhard, 16; Wikimedia Commons, 17 left; Wikimedia Commons, 17 right; © Memino/Shutterstock, 18; © Carlos E. Santa Maria/Shutterstock, 19; © Roberto Epifanio/Shutterstock, 20; © pablopicasso/Shutterstock, 21.



**Cherry Lake Press** is an imprint of Cherry Lake Publishing Group.

Library of Congress Cataloging-in-Publication Data

Names: Markovics, Joyce L., author.
Title: Inca mummies / by Joyce L Markovics.
Description: Ann Arbor, Michigan : Cherry Lake Publishing, [2021] | Series: Unwrapped : marvelous mummies | Includes bibliographical references and index. | Audience: Ages 8 | Audience: Grades 2-3
Identifiers: LCCN 2020030234 (print) | LCCN 2020030235 (ebook) | ISBN 9781534180437 (hardcover) | ISBN 9781534182141 (paperback) | ISBN 9781534183155 (ebook) | ISBN 9781534181441 (pdf)
Subjects: LCSH: Incas–Antiquities–Juvenile literature. | Mummies–Andes Region–Juvenile literature. | Excavations (Archaeology)–Andes Region–Juvenile literature.
Classification: LCC F3429.3.M8 M37 2020 (print) | LCC F3429.3.M8 (ebook) | DDC 985/.019–dc23
LC record available at https://lccn.loc.gov/2020030234
LC ebook record available at https://lccn.loc.gov/2020030235

Printed in the United States of America
Corporate Graphics

# CONTENTS

ICE MAIDEN 4

INCA MOUNTAIN MUMMIES 8

BUNDLED BODIES 14

MUMMIES EVERYWHERE! 18

Mummy Map 22
Glossary 23
Find Out More 24
Index 24
About the Author 24

# ICE MAIDEN

It was September 1995 in Peru. **Archaeologist** Johan Reinhard was exploring Mount Ampato in the Andes Mountains. As he neared the top, he saw objects scattered on the ground. There were shells, feathers, and a tiny statue. Then Johan spotted a cloth-wrapped bundle. When he took a closer look, he was stunned!

The Andes Mountains stretch all along the western coast of South America. Mount Ampato is 20,700 feet (6,309 meters) high!

Johan discovered the small frozen mummy of an Inca girl. The cold, dry mountain air had preserved the child's body for 500 years!

Johan Reinhard on Mount Ampato with the mummy bundle

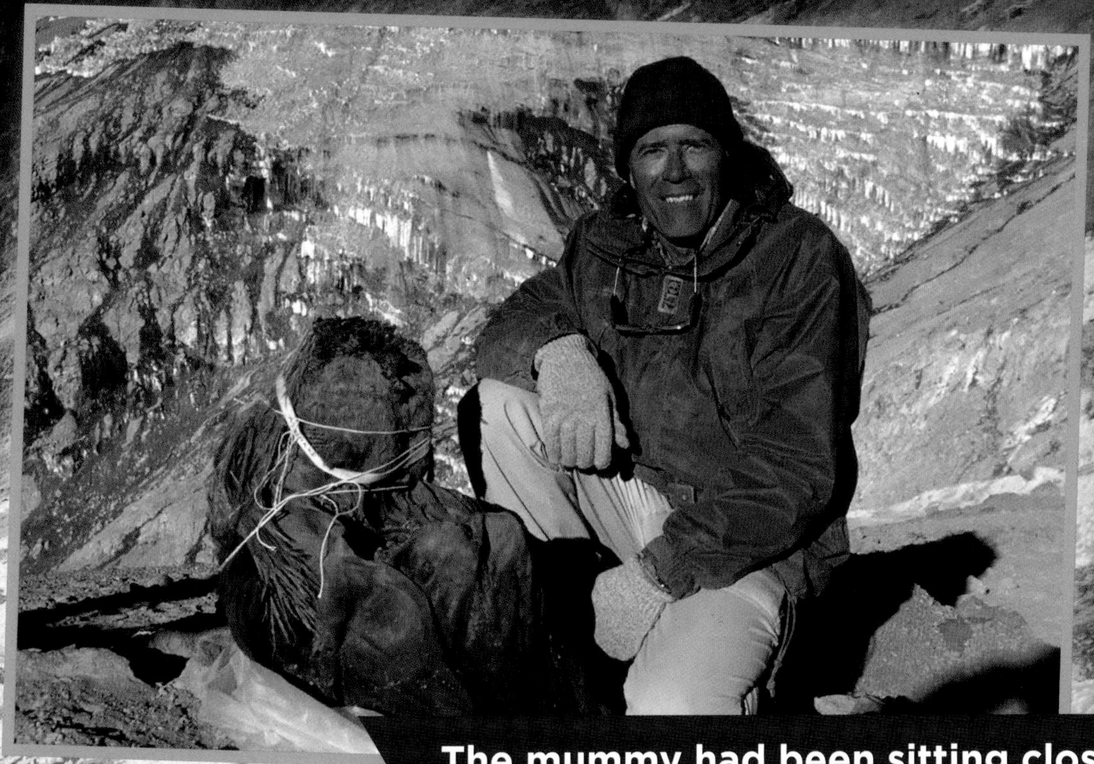

**The mummy had been sitting close to the top of the mountain. After a landslide, it tumbled down the slope.**

"A race against time had begun," said Johan. He knew that if he left the mummy on the mountain, she would deteriorate. So he strapped the 90-pound (41 kilograms) bundle to his back. He and his partner carried the body all the way down the mountain. The trip took 13 long hours.

Johan's climbing partner, Miguel Zárate, with the mummy bundle

The mummy would become known as Juanita (wah-NEE-tuh), or Ice Maiden. After arriving in a nearby city, Johan stored her in a freezer. Later, he and other scientists carefully studied every part of her. She was one of the best-preserved mummies the world had ever seen!

Mummy Juanita, the Ice Maiden

**Juanita was around 13 years old when she died.**

# INCA MOUNTAIN MUMMIES

Juanita is one of many Inca mountain mummies. Around 500 to 800 years ago, the Inca people built a large **empire** in South America. The empire stretched across the Andes Mountains.

The Incas **worshipped** sun and mountain gods. Sometimes, they made human **sacrifices** as a gift to the gods. Often, the sacrifices were done on top of icy mountains. Over 100 of these sites have been found on 30 different peaks. So how did the sacrificed bodies become mummies?

The ruler of the empire was called "the Inca." He was worshipped as a child of the sun god.

Machu Picchu (MAH-choo PEE-choo) is a town built by the Incas. *Machu Picchu* means "old mountain."

**The Inca Empire was destroyed in 1532 by an army from Spain.**

Usually, when a person dies, the body starts to **decay**. Chemicals and tiny living things called bacteria break down the **flesh**, such as the skin. However, in mummy bodies, the flesh has been preserved in some way.

A mummified body with preserved skin and hair

In the case of Inca mummies like Juanita, their bodies were frozen on mountaintops. In very cold and dry places, few bacteria live. This can slow down decay for hundreds, or even thousands, of years. Sometimes, ancient bodies look like they have been frozen in time.

Inca mummy cairns on mountain in Peru

Many Inca mummies were put in rocky pits, called cairns (KAIRNZ), on mountaintops. They were placed in a tucked position to face the rising sun.

The mountain mummies were often buried with tiny treasures. Gold, silver, and shell statues have been found near them. These items are thought to have been presents for the Inca gods.

A shell necklace and small statues found buried with Inca mummies

Some mummies were tightly wrapped in handmade textiles. Many had clothing and leather shoes. Sometimes, food, such as corn, was buried with the bundled bodies. By studying all these things, scientists learn about how the ancient Inca people lived.

A textile made by the Inca people

Corn was one of the main crops of the Inca people.

# BUNDLED BODIES

In 1999, Johan found three more Inca mummy children on Mount Llullaillaco (yoo-yeh-YAH-koh) in Argentina. Reaching them was not easy. It was cold and windy, and the burial pit lay under 5 feet (1.5 m) of rocky dirt. "We had to lower one of our workers into the pit by his ankles so he could pull [one] mummy out," said Johan.

The cairns on Mount Llullaillaco where the mummies were found

Once Johan reached the mummies, he was in awe. The 500-year-old children were even better preserved than Juanita. "The arms looked perfect, even down to visible hairs," he said.

One of the child mummies discovered on Mount Llullaillaco

**The child mummies froze before they dried out. As a result, their organs were intact. Frozen blood was found in one mummy's heart!**

The mummy children included two girls and a boy. They were between 8 and 14 years old when they died. One girl was wearing a beautiful feather head covering. The other girl had been struck by lightning after she was already dead! Her left shoulder was burnt, and an ear was missing. Other than that, the three bodies were in just about perfect condition, said Johan.

Johan and the girl mummy who had been burnt by lightning

He found beautiful **artifacts** around the bodies. There were small gold statues and a llama carved from a seashell. Johan thinks the children were probably human sacrifices like Juanita.

The white feather head covering and two small statues found with the child mummies

# MUMMIES EVERYWHERE!

Over 2,000 more Inca remains have been found in Puruchuco (poo-rooh-CHOO-ko) in Peru. Puruchuco is an ancient cemetery the size of five football fields! The burial ground dates from the 1400s.

Puruchuco cemetery

When archaeologists explored the cemetery, they found graves that held more than one person. Many were bundled. Some of the people were totally mummified, while others were mainly bones. Scientists still have a lot of work to do to find out who the people were and how they died.

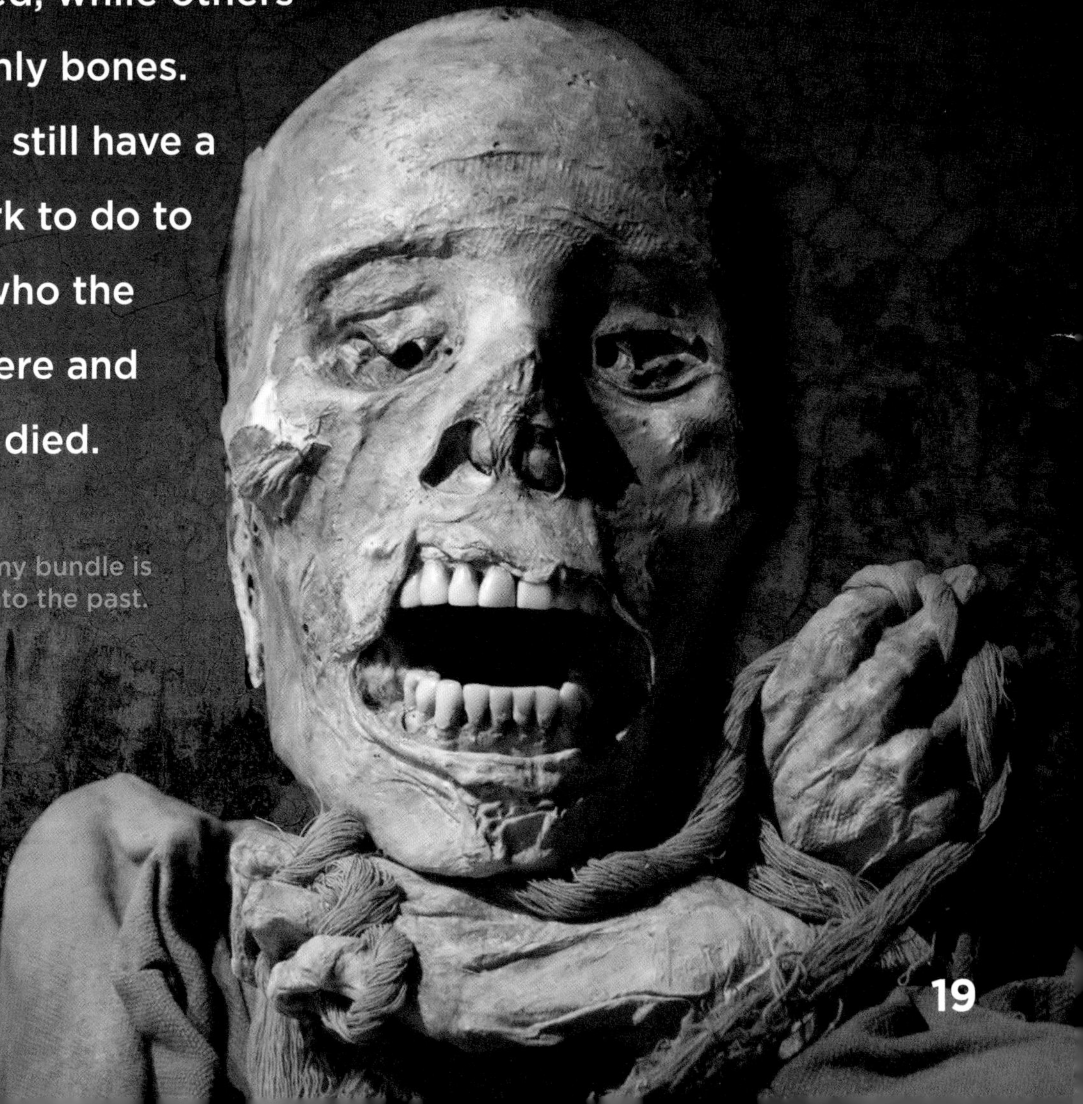

Each Inca mummy bundle is like a window into the past.

The Inca are also believed to have mummified their emperors. The Spanish tell stories of dead Inca emperors being carried through the streets. This was done on special occasions. One emperor mummy was "so well preserved he seemed alive," according to a report from the 1560s.

Descendents of the Inca people still celebrate their history. This parade honors the Inca sun god and emperor.

It's said that the emperor mummies were kept in palaces. They were dressed in fine clothing. Servants fed and cared for the mummies as if they were still alive!

What an Inca ruler's mummy might have looked like

# MUMMY MAP

**Puruchuco Cemetery**
1400s
Lima, Peru

**Juanita or Ice Maiden Mummy**
1500s
Mount Ampato, Peru

**Llullaillaco Mummies**
1500s
Mount Llullaillaco, Argentina

# GLOSSARY

**ancient** (AYN-shuhnt) very old

**archaeologist** (ahr-kee-AH-luh-jist) someone who studies the past by digging up and examining old things

**artifacts** (AHR-tuh-fakts) objects of historical interest that were made by people

**awe** (AW) a feeling of admiration and respect

**burial** (BER-ee-uhl) describing a place where dead bodies are put in the earth

**cemetery** (SEM-ih-ter-ee) an area of land where dead bodies are buried

**decay** (dih-KAY) to rot or break down

**deteriorate** (dih-TEER-ee-uh-rate) to get worse

**emperors** (EM-pur-urz) male rulers

**empire** (EM-pire) a large area that has the same ruler

**flesh** (FLESH) the soft part of a body that covers the bones

**maiden** (MAY-duhn) a young, unmarried woman

**organs** (OR-guhnz) body parts that do particular jobs inside the body

**palaces** (PAL-is-iz) grand homes of kings, queens, emperors, or other rulers

**preserved** (prih-ZURVD) protected something so that it stays in its original state

**sacrifices** (SAK-ruh-fise-iz) people or animals killed as part of a ceremony or as an offering to gods

**textiles** (TEK-stilez) fabrics or cloths that have been woven or knitted

**visible** (VIZ-uh-buhl) something that's able to be seen

**worshipped** (WUR-shipd) showed devotion to a god

# FIND OUT MORE

## Books

Carney, Elizabeth. *Mummies*. Washington, D.C.: National Geographic, 2009.

Martin, Michael. *Inca Mummies: Sacrifices and Rituals*. North Mankato, MN: Capstone Press, 2005.

Sloan, Christopher. *Mummies*. Washington, D.C.: National Geographic, 2010.

## Websites

**American Museum of Natural History: Mummies in Peru**
https://www.amnh.org/exhibitions/mummies/peru

**NOVA: Ice Mummies of the Inca**
https://www.pbs.org/wgbh/nova/peru

**Penn Museum: Frozen Mummies of the Andes**
https://www.penn.museum/sites/expedition/frozen-mummies-of-the-andes

# INDEX

archaeologists, 4, 19
Argentina, 14, 22
artifacts 12–13, 17
bacteria, 10–11
cairns, 11, 14
cemetery, 18–19
decay process, 10–11
emperors, 20–21
human sacrifices, 9, 17
Inca Empire, 8–9
Juanita or Ice Maiden Mummy, 4–7, 22
Mount Ampato, 4–7, 22
Mount Llullaillaco, 14–17, 22
mummy-making process, 10–11
palaces, 21
Peru, 4, 18, 22
Puruchuco cemetery, 18–19, 22
Reinhard, Johan, 4–7, 14–17

# ABOUT THE AUTHOR

**Joyce Markovics** digs mummies—and all kinds of curious things. She also loves learning about animals and people from the past and telling their stories.